Jedd

ANCIENT
GRECE

Leisure &
Community
Services

Please return this item by the last date stamped below, to the library from which it was borrowed.

Renewals
You may renew any item twice (for **3 weeks**) by telephone or post, providing it is not required by another reader. *Please quote the number stated below.*

Overdue charges
Please see library notices for the current rate of charges for overdue items. Overdue charges are not made on junior books unless borrowed on adult tickets.

Postage
Both adult and junior borrowers must pay any postage on overdue notices.

Heinemann

H www.heinemann.co.uk
Visit our website to find out more information about Heinemann books.

To order:
☎ Phone 44 (0) 1865 888020
📄 Send a fax to 44 (0) 1865 314091
💻 Visit the Heinemann Bookshop at www.heinemann.co.uk to browse our catalogue and order online.

First published in Great Britain by Heinemann Library, Halley Court, Jordan Hill, Oxford OX2 8EJ, a division of Reed Educational and Professional Publishing Ltd. Heinemann is a registered trademark of Reed Educational & Professional Publishing Ltd.

OXFORD MELBOURNE AUCKLAND JOHANNESBURG BLANTYRE
GABORONE IBADAN PORTSMOUTH (NH) USA CHICAGO

© Reed Educational and Professional Publishing Ltd 2001
The moral right of the proprietor has been asserted.

Designed by Celia Floyd
Originated by Dot Gradations
Printed in Hong Kong

05 04 03 02 01   05 04 03 02
10 9 8 7 6 5 4 3 2 1   10 9 8 7 6 5 4 3 2
ISBN 0 431 10205 8 (hardback)   ISBN 0 431 10214 7 (paperback)

British Library Cataloguing in Publication Data

Shuter, Jane
    Ancient Greece. – (Exploring history)
    1. Greece – History – To 146 B.C.   2. Greece – Civilization – To 146 B.C.
    3. Greece – Social conditions – To 146 B.C.
    I. Title
    938

Acknowledgements

The Publishers would like to thank the following for permission to reproduce photographs: AKG: Pg.6, Pg.11, Pg.18; Alinari-Giraudon: Pg.10; Ancient Art and Architecture: Pg.7, Pg.8, Pg.19, Pg.28; Bildarchive Preussicher Kulturbesitz: Pg.22; Chris Honeywell: Pg.23; Corbis: Pg.12, Pg.13, Pg.27; Empics: Pg.29; Hulton: Pg.20; National Tourist Organization of Greece: Pg.5; REPP/Heinemann – unknown: Pg.14; Richard Butcher & Magnet Harlequin: Pg.15, Pg.16, Pg.24 (both), Pg.25, Pg.26; Still Pictures: Pg.9; Werner Foreman Archive: Pg.17.

Cover photograph reproduced with permission of Michael Holford.

Every effort has been made to contact copyright holders of any material reproduced in this book. Any omissions will be rectified in subsequent printings if notice is given to the Publisher.

Any words appearing in the text in bold, **like this**, are explained in the glossary.

Contents

Where and when was ancient Greece?

The ancient Greek civilization lasted from about 800 BC, when the Greeks began to set up **city states**, to 146 BC when the Romans invaded Greece. Greece is a country broken up by mountains and the sea. About three-quarters of the land is mountains. Even today the rough land makes travel difficult. The ancient Greeks did not think of Greece as a single country – it had never been united by a single leader.

City states

The earliest Greeks chose a place with good farmland and settled down in small groups. The settlers could not farm the mountains, but they kept sheep and goats there in summer and collected honey from the bees. These groups traded with each other, but they also fought each other. Around 800 BC small groups began to join together into city states – a city and the land and villages surrounding it. The ideal city was built on a hill, with a good water supply, in the middle of fertile farmland. The city on the hill (**acropolis**) had walls built all around it. If the city state was attacked, all the people of the city crammed into the walled acropolis for safety.

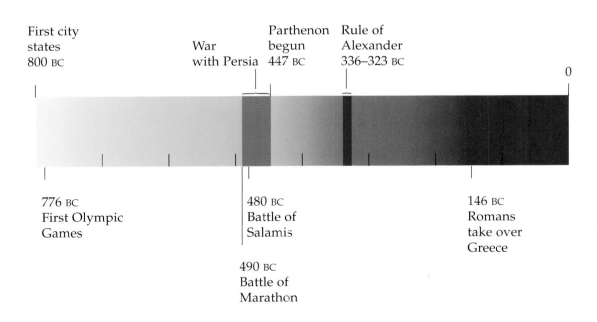

First city
states
800 BC

War
with Persia

Parthenon
begun
447 BC

Rule of
Alexander
336–323 BC

0

776 BC
First Olympic
Games

480 BC
Battle of
Salamis

146 BC
Romans
take over
Greece

490 BC
Battle of
Marathon

The landscape of Greece affected how it developed as a country. The mountains and the sea made travel dangerous and made it hard to form a single unified country.

Working together?

Some city states were small, with just a few hundred **citizens**, others had thousands of citizens. Big city states were the most powerful and tried to control weaker neighbours.

Although city states were run in different ways, all Greeks spoke the same language and worshipped the same gods. They might fight each other, but when enemies from outside Greece, such as the Persians, attacked, the city states joined together to fight them.

 Aristotle, an Athenian **philosopher**, wrote that the size of a city state was important:

You can't have a city state of ten citizens. But when you have 100,000 citizens it is no longer a city state. It has to be big enough to run itself. But it has to be small enough for the citizens to know each other. Otherwise how can they choose officials?

 ## Exploring further

The Heinemann Explore CD-ROM will give you information about Ancient Greece. From the Contents screen you can click on the blue words to find out about the ancient Greeks and their lives.

What were the similarities and differences between Athens and Sparta?

Athens and Sparta were the most powerful **city states** in ancient Greece. They shared the same language and religion. In both city states all the men had to fight in times of war. In other ways they were very different.

Government

At first both Athens and Sparta were ruled by kings. Then both were ruled by 'oligarchies' – small groups of powerful people. Sparta remained an oligarchy, run by a small, powerful warrior group, the Spartiates. Most Spartans were either Perioeci (**citizens** who paid taxes, served in the army and were protected by Spartan laws) or Helots (people from lands conquered and ruled by Sparta who had no rights).

Athens came to be ruled 'by the people' as a **democracy**. It was run by a council of 500 officials, chosen each year by **lot**. Laws were passed by an **Assembly** of all Athenian citizens. The council made sure the laws were carried out and the city state was run properly.

Who could vote?

Athenian democracy was not like modern democracy. Only citizens over 18 could vote. Women, **slaves** and foreigners could not become citizens. So democracy in Athens meant rule by the men of Athens.

 Greek democracy

This carving from ancient Athens shows Democracy, standing, crowning 'the people' – an Athenian man.

Attitudes to outsiders

Athenians traded with city states not dependent on Athens, as well as countries outside Greece. Many Athenians made trade **goods**, including beautifully decorated vases. In contrast the Spartans had as little to do with other city states as possible.

Great thinkers?

Athens is the city state we know the most about for several reasons. Athenians believed in education; in writing and recording; in plays, poetry and in books of all kinds. This means there is a lot of written evidence left for us to study. Trade made Athens rich, which meant that there was money to spare to build beautiful public buildings. There is far less evidence from Sparta for us to use to understand how it was run since the Spartans did not value education or the written word in the same way.

This Spartan statue shows a man in armour. We know that the rulers of Sparta were warriors and that they thought the most important thing a person could do was to become a good fighter.

Exploring further

You can discover more about the government of Athens on the CD-ROM. Follow this path:

Contents > Exploring > Change and Influences > Government

Family life

Athenians and Spartans had very different views on family life. They agreed that the man was the head of the household, but whereas in Athens family life was seen as important, in Sparta it was not. In Athens women ran the home and brought up children. Women were not expected to go out in public much, unless they were poor or slaves. While there was a lot of emphasis on Athenian men keeping fit, this was not expected of women.

In Sparta everyone, both men and women, was expected to exercise and keep fit. Women were not as confined to the home. The home was less important. Boys left home at the age of seven and lived in **barracks** with other young men until they were 30 years old, when they could set up a home if they wanted to. Even then, they were expected to spend a lot of time at the barracks. Army life was more important than family life.

 Plutarch wrote about how Spartans bring up their babies and children:

The father brought the new-born baby for the leaders to examine. If they thought it was strong and healthy they let it live. If it was weak or deformed it was taken to an open place and left to die. Children had to eat what they were given, or not eat at all. They were not allowed night-lights; they were expected not to be afraid of the dark.

This Spartan statue shows a girl running. Spartan women were expected to exercise and keep healthy, so as to have strong and healthy children.

The **Acropolis** of Athens had high stone walls and beautiful marble temples, built to last.

City life

Athens was a city with lots of beautiful public buildings, shops and public baths. Most ordinary people lived in quite simple homes, built from mud brick, but wealthy people had beautifully decorated homes. Athenians mostly ate simply, but male dinner parties often had lots of wine and rich food.

Spartan buildings were all made from mud brick. The only stone building so far discovered is a very simple temple to the goddess Athena. We do not think that Spartans had public baths. People washed each day in a basin of water. Spartan food was simple and they drank only a little alcohol. Almost any kind of comfort was seen as a luxury that would 'soften up' warriors – so it was a bad thing.

Exploring further

We know more about Athens than we do about Sparta, because more writings have survived. Follow this path to find what Xenophon, an Athenian, wrote about Sparta:

Contents > Written Sources > Early Spartan laws on marriage

What made ancient Greek fighters so powerful?

The ancient Greeks were very fierce fighters. The big Persian invasions of 490 BC and 480 BC were both beaten back, even though the Persian army was far bigger than the Greek one. Why?

Practice

Greek **city states** often fought each other. They did not have permanent armies, but their men kept fit, and had well-maintained weapons and armour. Greeks who lived on the islands or in coastal city states also knew the waters of their part of the Mediterranean very well. This was useful in sea battles. From 490 BC onwards, Athens kept a navy to protect Greece, paid for by yearly contributions by many city states.

Patriotism

All the men of a city state fought in the army. They were proud of their city state. Their homes and families were at risk if they were beaten. The Persians often used soldiers taken from conquered countries, who did not want to fight and had no loyalty to Persia. They also used paid **mercenaries** who stopped fighting if they did not get their money.

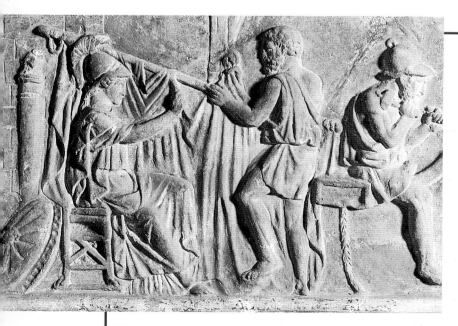

Ships were an important part of everyday life for the ancient Greeks and often came into the stories they told as well. Here the goddess Athena is helping the hero Jason to get his ship ready, from the story of Jason and the Golden Fleece.

 These Greek soldiers are putting on armour made from several layers of stiffened linen cloth. This was much lighter and cooler than metal armour, although it did not give as much protection. The helmets and shields are made from metal and wood.

Tactics

The ancient Greeks had developed very efficient fighting tactics. Most Greek soldiers were **hoplites** who fought on foot, armed with spears and swords. They often fought in a **phalanx** pattern, side by side with their shields overlapping to make a wall. Each phalanx was about six men deep. If hoplites in the front row were killed, others stepped forward from the row behind to take their place. This tactic worked best in defence, so Greeks seldom attacked. They used their knowledge of the land to choose a good place to defend, then formed a phalanx and waited for the enemy to attack.

Armour as evidence

Hoplites wore helmets and carried shields for protection. They also wore armour that covered their chests and back. **Archaeologists** can study armour that has survived. A shield survived in a burial so well that archaeologists could work out exactly how it was made and make a **reconstruction**. They saw that the shield was designed to fit over the shoulder; something they could not have worked out from writings or vase paintings.

 ### Exploring further

Look on the CD-ROM for information about some of the great battles of ancient Greece. Follow this path:
Contents > Exploring > Invasion and Warfare
Click on the words Marathon, Thermopylae and Salamis to find out about these famous battles.

Was the battle of Marathon a great victory for the ancient Greeks?

In 490 BC a Persian army of about 200,000 landed on the Greek coast, near Athens. Athens and the nearby **city state** of Plataea raised 10,000 soldiers. The Athenians sent a runner to Sparta to ask for help. The Spartans said they would come after their big religious festival, which lasted several days. By the time they arrived, it was all over.

What happened at the battle of Marathon?

The Athenians and Persians camped at either end of the plain of Marathon. The Greeks were outnumbered and had no horsemen or **archers**. They knew the Persians put their best soldiers in the centre front in battle. So they decided to put the best Greek soldiers on the sides and make a surprise attack (Greek armies seldom attacked). The Persians were shocked when the Greeks attacked at a run. The Persians broke through the Greeks at the front, but the strong Greek soldiers broke through both sides of the Persian army and attacked them from behind. The Persians fled. About 64,000 Persians were killed and only 192 Greeks.

Painted evidence

A Persian archer on the wall of a temple. Neither the archers nor the horsemen were much use to the Persians at the battle of Marathon.

The Greek soldiers who died at Marathon were buried in a grave all together. There is now a modern monument to mark where they are buried.

Was Marathon a great victory?

The Greek victory at Marathon stopped the Persian invasion of Greece. Not only did the Greeks win, but they won despite being heavily outnumbered and their losses were small compared to the losses of the Persians. All these things make Marathon look like a great victory.

But there was at least one bad consequence of the battle of Marathon – a lack of trust between Athens and Sparta. Greek city states had always helped each other against outside enemies. The Spartans felt they had to refuse to help – for religious reasons. The Athenians felt the Spartans used their festival as an excuse and wanted to make the Athenians fight alone.

Pheidippides

Pheidippides was the runner sent by the Athenians to Sparta, about 120 kilometres away. He got there in just two days, despite having to run on narrow, dusty, mountainous roads. He then had to run all the way back with their refusal. Long races are now called marathons. Some people think this comes from Pheidippides' run; others think it comes from the much shorter distance (41 kilometres) run to bring the news of the victory at Marathon to Athens. The modern Olympic marathon is run over 42 kilometres.

Exploring further

The CD-ROM gives more details of the Battle of Marathon. Follow this path to read a story about King Darius of Persia:
Contents > Written Sources > A story told at about the time of Marathon
Follow the link on page 11 to read more about the battle itself.

Who did the ancient Greeks worship and why?

A happy family?

The ancient Greeks believed in many different gods and goddesses. They believed the twelve most important gods and goddesses lived on Mount Olympus. They were a family and, just like a human family, they argued as well as looking after each other. Zeus, the most important, had the final say in everything. His wife, Hera, was the goddess of marriage and childbirth. His brother, Poseidon, was god of the sea. One of Zeus' sisters, Demeter, made the crops grow. The other, Hestia, took care of the home. The other seven gods and goddesses were Zeus' children by different mothers. They were: Athena, goddess of wisdom; Apollo, god of light and music; Hermes, messenger of the gods; Aphrodite, goddess of beauty and love; Hephaistos, god of metalwork and Ares, god of war. Sometimes gods had several names, depending on the powers they were using. So, Athena, as Athena Nike, was the goddess of victory. She and Ares might disagree over who was to win a battle or war.

Athena

A **reconstruction** of the statue of Athena made for the Parthenon in Athens.

The gods were put in an inner room in the temple, but when the doors were opened the statues could 'see' outside to where presents or **sacrifices** were left for them.

Keeping gods and goddesses happy

The ancient Greeks believed their gods and goddesses controlled everyday life and could come to Earth to change it. So it was important to please the gods; happy gods helped you, but unhappy gods punished you. People had special places in their homes where they could pray to the gods. There were also public **shrines** in all sorts of places where people could pray or leave presents. But they needed a way to show the gods how important they were.

So the Greeks built temples for their gods. Temples were not, like modern places of worship, for ordinary people to pray in. They were homes for statues of the gods, which were cared for by priests as if they were the gods. Religious ceremonies and festivals went on outside the temple. The Greeks believed the work they put into the temple and time they spent worshipping would please the gods. Big religious festivals could last several days and include sport and theatre performances.

Exploring further

You can discover much more about Greek beliefs on the CD-ROM. Follow this path:

Contents > Exploring > Beliefs

What happened at the theatre?

Almost every Greek city had a theatre because plays were part of many religious festivals. There was an **altar** in the orchestra, the main acting space, for **sacrifices**. At first, theatres were only used for festivals. Plays were either spoken or sung in rhyme.

What did a theatre look like?

Greek theatres were open air and circular. About three quarters of the stage and orchestra were surrounded by seats. The only part of the circle with no seats around it was the area behind the stage. The orchestra took up most of the circular acting space, while the stage was a raised section behind it.

Did women go to the theatre?

There is no evidence left from the time that tells us. We know actors were men and that women kept apart from men, especially in Athens. But plays were part of festivals, so women probably went, but sat in a separate section. We know women went to the Olympics, but had their own games and could not watch the men competing.

This theatre is the ancient Greek theatre in Athens. The photo was taken from the walls of the **Acropolis**. It was near the temples because it was used for religious festivals.

Costume

This carving shows the playwright Menander looking at a collection of theatrical masks. These masks have hair attached, so the actors would not need separate wigs.

What were plays like?

The chorus stood in the orchestra. The chorus was about fifteen people who all spoke together, telling the story and making comments on what was happening. One or two of them might play musical instruments, but they were not musicians like a modern orchestra. The actors stood on the stage and spoke the big speeches for the main characters. Only three actors – all men – could be on stage at once. They changed character by changing masks that showed many faces, young and old, male and female.

How did theatres change?

Plays developed into tragedies and comedies. Tragedies re-told old myths and legends about the gods. Often, things turned out unhappily. Comedies were funny. They made fun of people and had everyday storylines. They were often rude, too. Dwarves often played servants. With their red wigs and white masks they were the earliest sort of circus clown. By the end of the ancient Greek period, plays were being performed more often.

Exploring further

Greek plays are still performed today. Follow this path on the CD-ROM to read more about the theatre and to see a picture of a Greek play being performed:
Contents > Exploring > Change and Influences > The theatre
Click on the pictures on the left of the screen to make them bigger.

What do the sources tell us about the importance of the Olympics to the ancient Greeks?

To us, the Olympic games are a series of sporting events. Countries send teams to compete and people support their country. But the ancient Greek Olympics were part of a religious event. Sacred **heralds** announced when the games were due. **City states** had to agree not to fight each other for a month before and after the games, to allow competitors and spectators to get to Olympia, where the games were always held. The sources on these pages are all about the ancient Olympic games.

Source 1

Modern historians H D Amos and A G P Lang describe the visitors to Olympia:

Spectators came in their thousands; and with them came all the sorts of people who have attended fairs in every age and country: drink-sellers, showmen, pastry-cooks, gamblers, peddlers, thieves, singers, prostitutes, travelling actors. One account says: 'Writers were reading their rubbish aloud. Many poets were reciting their verses to the applause of others, many conjurers were showing off their tricks, fortune-tellers theirs.'

Source 2

A vase painting of wrestling at the Olympics.

Source 3

A vase painting of an Olympic chariot race.

Day 1: religious ceremonies, including sacrifices to Zeus; taking of oaths and checking of athletes
Day 2: horse racing, chariot racing, pentathlon
Day 3: religious ceremonies all morning, then boys' events
Day 4: 'track' events, wrestling, boxing, **pankration**, racing in armour
Day 5: religious ceremonies, banquets, sacrifices

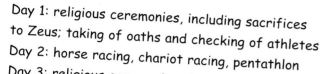

Source 4

Events at the Olympics.

Source 5

Pausanias, a Greek writer and traveller in about AD 150, described one pankration event.

Arrachion's opponent caught him, holding him with his legs in a powerful scissors grip. He started to strangle Arrachion, who, with the last of his strength, reached out and broke one of his opponent's toes. Arrachion died of the strangling. But, at the same time, the strangler gave in, because of the pain in his toe. So Arrachion was proclaimed the winner and crowned with the olive garland.

Exploring further

To find more information about the Olympics, click on Search on the top panel of the Contents page. Pick Olympic Games from the keywords on the next page and click on Enter. The screen will now show a list of pages on the CD-ROM that mention the Games. Click on the names of the pages to find out what they show.

How have the ancient Greeks influenced our language?

We use Greek every day. Greek is one of the languages that English is based on. Many of the words we use, especially words to do with education, maths and science come from Greek words. Viking words in our language are words for basic things such as sky, bread and window. Greek words are mostly to do with ideas.

One Greek word that we use is 'alphabet', from alpha and beta, the first two letters of the Greek alphabet. The Greek alphabet is not exactly like ours, although some things are similar.

ΕΞΗΛΘΕΝΔΕ ΒΑCΙΛΕΥCCΟΔΟΜωΝΕΙCΥΝΑΝ
ΤΗCΙΝ ΑΥΤωΜΕΤΑΤΟΫ ΠΟCΤΡΕΨΑΙΑΥΤΟΝ
ΑΠΟΤΗC ΚΟΠΗCΤΟΥΧΟΔΑΛΛΟΤΟ ΜΟΡΚΑ
ΤωΝΒΑCΙΛΕωΝΤωΝΜΕΤΑΥΤΟΥΕΙCΤΗ
ΚΟΙΛΑΔΑ ΤΗΝCΑΥΗ·ΤΟΥΤΟΗΝΤΟΠΕΔΙΟΝ
ΒΑCΙΛΕωΝ· ΚΑΙΜΕΛΧΙCΕΔΕΚΒΑCΙΛΕΥC
CΑΛΗΜΕΞΗΝΕΓΚΕΝΑΡΤΟΥCΚΑΙΟΙΝΟΝΗ
ΔΕΪΕΡΕΥCΤΟΥΘΥΤΟΥΥΨΙCΤΟΥ· ΚΑΙΕΥΛΟΓ
CΕΝΤΟΝΑΒΡΑΜ ΚΑΙΕΙΠΕΝ· ΕΥΛΟΓΗΜΕΝΟC

 One of the earliest examples of ancient Greek writing. This is written entirely in capitals, without the spacing or punctuation that we use in modern writing.

The Greek alphabet

Capital	Lower-case	Greek name	English
A	α	Alpha	a
B	β	Beta	b
Γ	γ	Gamma	g
Δ	δ	Delta	d
E	ε	Epsilon	e
Z	ζ	Zeta	z
H	η	Eta	e
Θ	θ	Theta	th
I	ι	Iota	i
K	κ	Kappa	k
Λ	λ	Lambda	l
M	μ	Mu	m
N	ν	Nu	n
Ξ	ξ	Xi	x
O	ο	Omnicron	o
Π	π	Pi	p
P	ρ	Rho	r
Σ	σ	Sigma	s
T	τ	Tau	t
Y	υ	Upsilon	u
Φ	φ	Phi	ph
X	χ	Chi	ch
Ψ	ψ	Psi	ps
Ω	ω	Omega	o

Exploring further

Discover more English words that use ancient Greek language on the CD-ROM. Follow this path:

Contents > Exploring > Change and Influences > Language

What similarities are there between ancient Greek schools and our schools?

The way children were educated was different in each **city state**. Education was different for boys and girls. Boys were educated to be good **citizens** and take part in the public life of the city state. Girls were educated in housekeeping and how to look after a family. Modern boys' and girls' education is no longer different. As you read about how schools worked think about the similarities and differences between schools then and now.

What should children learn?

In some city states, Sparta for instance, reading and writing were unimportant. Boys learned to be good fighters, though children of tradesmen also learned their father's trade. In Athens citizens had to be educated to take part in voting in the **Assembly**. They had to be able to listen to a speech and think about several sides of an argument. Athenian boys also went to 'wrestling school' each day, to learn many sports, not just wrestling. They had to be fit, to fight in the army.

A vase painting of a lesson going on, with school equipment in use and hung on the walls.

 In schools today classes are larger and boys and girls work together.

School times

From 7–14 boys went to school each morning and learned to read, write and do simple maths. They worked in small groups in one room, which had stools or benches, but no desks. Pupils read aloud and learned poetry by heart. In the afternoons they went to wrestling schools. At the age of 14, children of tradesmen began to learn a trade. The children of rich Athenians went to the Assembly, the market place and the gymnasium to watch, listen to and learn from the older men. From about 400 BC boys from 14 upwards were taught to debate by specialist teachers.

Equipment

Schoolboys in ancient Greece relied more on memory than we do today and did not need much school equipment. When they needed to, they wrote on wooden boards covered with a layer of wax. They used a wooden pen called a stylus with a sharp end for writing and a flat end for 'rubbing out'. The wax was melted and re-applied from time to time.

Exploring further

Try searching for information about Greek schools, using the keyword Education. You can find out how to search the CD-ROM in the box on page 19.

How have the ancient Greeks influenced our buildings?

All the ancient Greek buildings that have survived and influenced modern building styles are public buildings. The ancient Greeks wanted their public buildings, especially temples to the gods, to be beautiful. They saw a beautiful building as one that was **symmetrical** and in proportion. They worked to a mathematical **ratio**. The Victorians liked this 'balanced' building style and copied it for their public buildings.

Building styles

Ancient Greek architects had not worked out how to build arches or curved roofs. So their buildings were made up of upright columns supporting a flat roof. A sloping roof could then be built on top of the flat one, to carry away rainwater. Columns were built from a series of drum shapes on top of each other. These were made without **mortar** at the joins. When the buildings were finished they looked as if they had been made from a single piece of stone. The columns were decorated when they were finished. Fine 'fluting' grooves in various widths were made down the whole length of the column.

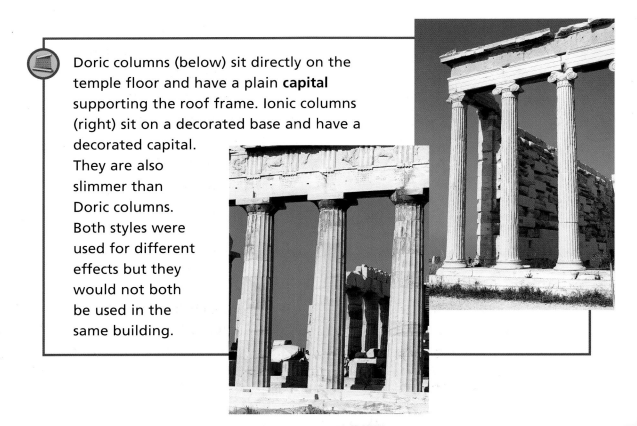

Doric columns (below) sit directly on the temple floor and have a plain **capital** supporting the roof frame. Ionic columns (right) sit on a decorated base and have a decorated capital. They are also slimmer than Doric columns. Both styles were used for different effects but they would not both be used in the same building.

The Parthenon, on the **Acropolis** of Athens, shows how the Greeks' use of mathematical ratio worked. Distance (A) is four-ninths the width of the Parthenon (B). The width of each column (C) is four-ninths the distance between them (D).

Building 'tricks'

The ancient Greeks worked very hard to make sure that their buildings looked right. They knew that people's eyes may play tricks on them, so they made sure to allow for this. They were prepared to build crooked, so that people would see straight. Columns are narrower at the top than at the bottom. If they just get slowly narrower, our eyes see a dip inwards about two-thirds of the way up. So the ancient Greeks made their columns bulge a bit at just that point, to make them look perfectly smooth. For the same reason, they made the floor slightly higher in the centre of the building and made the columns tilt slightly inward towards the roof.

Exploring further

The CD-ROM contains lots of information about the Acropolis, one of the most important buildings in ancient Greece. Follow this path:
Contents > Digging Deeper > The Acropolis
Click on the words in blue to explore further.

How have the ancient Greeks influenced our knowledge and ideas?

We use ancient Greek ideas in many ways in modern life. Many of the basic principles of mathematics and science were first discovered by ancient Greeks. Here are just some examples of areas of our lives affected by ancient Greek thinking.

Politics

The Athenian idea of **democracy** has influenced a lot of political thinkers. Many modern countries run themselves as democracies. Democracy comes from the Greek words 'demos' [the people] and 'kratia' [rule]. Democracy has come to mean some kind of elected government, although who can vote varies. In Athens all male **citizens** over 18 could vote.

Herodotus

The word 'history' comes from the Greek word for enquiry. The ancient Greeks, like the historian Herodotus (right), were the first to want to record the past as accurately as possible and interpret it.

Mathematics

The Greek **philosopher** Plato said 'God is always doing **geometry**'. The ancient Greeks were fascinated by mathematical ideas, especially geometry and **algebra**. One of the most famous Greek mathematical thinkers was Pythagoras whose many mathematical ideas we use today.

An ancient Greek carving of a doctor examining a patient.

Hippocrates

Hippocrates was a doctor who collected together the writings of many Greek doctors. He is often called 'the father of medicine' because of this and his name is given to the **oath** that doctors had to take well into the twentieth century – the Hippocratic Oath.

Medicine and health

The ancient Greeks believed it was important to eat well, exercise and get plenty of sleep to be healthy, just as we do now. They also believed that it was important to keep homes and clothes clean and that the government should provide a clean water supply. Ancient Greek medical ideas had a big influence on modern medicine. The idea of 'clinical observation' (making notes on a patient's progress and using these notes to understand disease) is how doctors work now. The Greeks were also the first people we know to have set down rules about how doctors should behave.

Maps

The ancient Greeks made careful observations and drew maps of both the Earth and the sky. They developed the lines of latitude and longitude we use on maps now. Heracleitus mapped the planets, listing them in their correct order from Earth. Eratosthenes calculated that the Earth was 40,000 kilometres around. He was only 67 kilometres out!

Exploring further

You can discover more about Greek thinkers in the Biographies section of the CD-ROM. Contents > Biographies
Click on the names of the thinkers to find out more. There are biographies of Archimedes, Herodotus, Socrates and many others.

In what ways are the modern Olympic games like the ancient ones?

When, why and for how long were the ancient Olympics held?

You have already seen how the ancient Olympic games were held for religious reasons. They were held every four years, just like our modern Olympics. The games were so important that even if two **city states** were fighting at the time of the Olympics they stopped while the games were held. The games lasted five days, although half of the time was taken up with religious ceremonies.

Who competed?

Athletes competed as individuals. City states did not send teams to the games, although they shared the glory if someone from their city state won. Athletes had to pay their own expenses, by taking part in 'paid' games run at other times. In this sense, ancient athletes were 'professionals', not **amateurs** like modern competitors.

What events are there?

Modern and ancient Olympic events include running, throwing and jumping events of various kinds. Other events are different, because the technology of the modern world is different. Also, the modern games last for longer, so more events can be included.

Ancient sports

Field sports, like discus throwing, remain an important part of the Olympic games today.

The marathon race is still run at the Olympic games. This is the Sydney 2000 games.

How did they win?

Modern athletes have to compete on the day to win. Ancient Greek athletes could win 'without dust'. This meant their opposition took one look at them and gave in. This was seen as a good way to win.

What did they win?

Just like modern athletes, ancient Greek athletes were competing for glory, rather than money. Modern athletes win a gold, silver or bronze medal but no prize money. In ancient Greece the only reward was a crown of olive leaves, given to the person who came first.

Baron Pierre de Coubertin

Baron de Coubertin (1863–1937) was a French aristocrat. He was the person who pushed for starting the Olympic games again. The first modern Olympics were held in 1896 in Athens – the capital city of Greece, the country that gave birth to the Olympics.

Exploring further

Follow this path to discover what happened at the ancient Olympic Games:
Contents > Exploring > Change and Influences > The Olympics
Click on the pictures on the left of the screen to explore links between the ancient and modern Olympics.

Timeline

800 BC	First city states set up
c.700 BC	Homer writes *The Iliad* and *The Odyssey*
735 BC	City of Rome set up
776 BC	First Olympic games
600 BC	Greek city states had set up over 1500 colonies around the Mediterranean
c.530 BC	Pythagoras writes about mathematical ideas
509 BC	Rome becomes a Republic
490 BC	Persians invade Greece – Battle of Marathon
480 BC	Persians invade again – Battles of Thermopylae and Salamis
450 BC	Athens at the height of its power
c.450 BC	Hippocrates works as a doctor
447 BC	Building of the Parthenon begins
c.440 BC	Herodotus writes his histories
c.420 BC	Socrates begins teaching philosophy
400 BC	Sparta at the height of its power
c.400 BC	Plato begins writing about perfect governments
336 BC	Alexander the Great becomes king of Macedonia
334 BC	Alexander the Great invades Persia
332 BC	Alexander the Great takes over Egypt
331 BC	City of Alexandria built, later to become a centre of learning and invention
325 BC	Alexander's fleet explores the Indian Ocean
323 BC	Alexander the Great dies
310 BC	Romans begin to conquer an empire, spreading through Italy from Rome
250–212 BC	Archimedes inventing
146 BC	Romans take over Greece

Glossary

acropolis   a hilltop fortress in ancient Greece

Acropolis   the name used for the hilltop fortress of Athens

algebra   a branch of maths invented by the Greeks, which uses Greek letters to represent numbers and relationships between numbers

altar   a special table in a temple or church for religious ceremonies

amateurs   people who do something for fun, not pay

archaeologist   a person who digs up and studies things from the past

archers   warriors who shoot arrows

Assembly   the assembly of Athens where all the citizens gathered to vote on laws or actions

barracks   a large building or group of buildings, for housing soldiers

capital   head of a pillar or column

citizens   men over 18 born in a city to parents who were citizens. Citizens had rights in their own city but not in any other.

city state   a city and the land it controls around it

democracy   'rule by the people' – this is when ordinary people get to take part in running the country

geometry   maths which is about shapes and their movements

goods   things made to trade or sell

herald   someone who announces by music or voice someone or something important

hoplites   soldiers who fought on foot with spears

lot   a method of deciding something by random selection

mercenaries   a professional soldier hired by another country for money

mortar   a mixture of cement, sand and water, which sets hard when dry

oath   a formal promise made in the name of a god or person

pankration   an Olympic contest of hand-to-hand combat

phalanx   a tight formation

philosopher   someone who studies ideas

ratio   the relationship of one figure or number to another

reconstruction   using evidence to make something like the original lost or damaged item

sacrifice   offering something to the gods

shrines   a small religious site, sometimes for one god or saint

slaves   people who are owned, like property, by their masters

symmetrical   the same on both sides of a middle point creating a balanced look

Index